If...

# If...

## (Questions for the Game of Life)

Evelyn McFarlane & James Saywell
Illustrations by James Saywell

Villard/New York

ISBN: 0-679-44535-8
Library of Congress cataloging-in-publication information is available.

Manufactured in the United States of America on acid-free paper.
98765432

First Edition

Produced by March Tenth, Inc.

If...

**If** is the ultimate book about fantasy. Each of its questions is meant to spark and tantalize the imagination. They are a celebration of the human spirit, which loves to dream and needs to hope, but which can also fear and even grow angry. Our ability to imagine is the remarkable gift we have been given to lead us into joy and aspiration and out of despair or sadness, because common to all of us is the idea that there could be a different world, perhaps a better one.

How many times a day do we say, "If only . . ."? If we could create the perfect life, the perfect city, the perfect home, the perfect job, the perfect mate. We all fantasize, and we all dream. We dream of perfection, money, revenge, glory, change. We fantasize about both good and evil, about winning and losing, about our past and future. Fantasies are what inspire us all; to work, marry, raise families, create, improve our world. It is why we lose ourselves in books, go to movies, watch television, go to the ballgame and on vacation. We dreamed as children and we dream now because without our fantasies we would be lost. We imagine in order to learn, to understand, to strive, to attempt, to predict, to avoid, to correct, to describe, to solve.

This book is also a game. It was born of many dinner parties and gatherings, when just to throw out a provocative question and ask for each person's answer always led to the most surprising and fascinating discussions. Every time, a kind of synergetic and addictive momentum took over as answers led to other related questions, reasons were demanded, disagreements were unleashed, conditions were imposed, other's answers were predicted, and inevitably those involved were startled by the responses, at times even their

3

own. No matter who is present it seems to be irresistible, whether we are at a flagging party, on a long car or plane ride, among a group of students, within a family, or alone with someone very close to us. It is infectious and fascinating to watch and take part in.

Of course implicit in every question is "why?" In some sense it is like taking the pulse of a moment in time, or a group of friends, to see what we believe in; to see what world we envision. Whether they are read randomly or in sequence, the responses these questions elicit can lead to extraordinary offshoots; other related questions will occur, and variations on these, and attached caveats and conditions "customize" the original list depending on who is there to play. Because everybody, old or young, fat or thin, intelligent or not, from one culture or another, has the ability and inclination to wonder.

And so, aside from the truths that are revealed, the contemplation that is provoked, the confidence or anxiety that surfaces, the self-knowledge that results, or the understanding that might be gained, above all we hope that asking these questions inspires optimism, since no matter who or what we really are, we share the ability to travel together the unpredictable journey of the imagination, which leads us through the wonderful game of life.

If you were to be granted one wish, what would it be?

If you could spend one whole night alone with anyone in the world who is currently alive, who would you select?

＋・＝＋＝・＋

If you could spend one whole night alone with anyone in history, who would you choose?

＋・＝＋＝・＋

If you could physically transport yourself to any place in the world at this moment, where would you go?

**If** you could have lived through any war in history (without actually fighting in it), which would it be?

—— ⚎◆⚎ ——

**If** you could eliminate any one type of insect permanently from the earth, what would you get rid of?

—— ⚎◆⚎ ——

**If** you had to eliminate a single type of animal forevermore, which would you choose?

**If** you could have an elegant dinner alone with anyone presently alive, whether you know them or not, who would you want it to be?

If you could alter one physical characteristic of your mate, what would you change?

---

If you could dine alone with anyone from any period in history, which person would it be?

---

If you could, in retrospect, change one thing about your childhood, what would it be?

---

If you could have any room in the world become your bedroom from now on, which room would you choose?

If you could change one thing in the world right now, what would you alter?

---

If you had to assassinate one famous person who is alive right now, who would it be, and how would you do it?

---

If you could permanently alter one thing about your physical appearance, what would you change?

---

If you could have stopped aging at any point in your life up to the present, how old would you want to remain?

8

If you could inherit a comfortable home in any city in the world that you could use but not sell, where would you want it to be?

---

If you could inherit a vacation home anywhere in the world in which you could spend one month a year, but that you could never sell, where would it be?

If you could suddenly possess an extraordinary talent in one of the arts, what would you like it to be?

---

If you could be instantly fluent in one other language that you currently do not read or speak, which would it be?

9

If you could have permanent possession of any single object in the world, what would you want it to be?

If you could have had the starring role in one film already made, which movie would you pick?

If you could return for one year to one age in your life, knowing what you know now, to relive that year as you wish, which year would you go back to?

If you had to identically repeat any single year of your life to date, without changing a thing, which year would you relive?

If you could be sculpted by any artist in history, who would you choose?

If you were to have your entire wardrobe designed for you by a single clothing designer for the rest of your life, who would you select?

If you were to be stranded forever on a desert island and could have only one book to read, which would you want?

If you could say one sentence to the current pope, what would it be?

If you could have one person from history live his or her full life over again, starting now, who would you pick?

---

If you could have personally witnessed one event in history, what would you want to have seen?

---

If one of your parents was to be a famous person from any time in history, who would you want them to be?

---

If you could receive one small package this very moment, who would it be from and what would be in it?

12

If you could own one painting from any collection in the world but were not allowed to sell it, which work of art would you select?

---

If you could have chosen your own first name, other than your current one, what would it be?

---

If you could have seduced one person that you knew in your lifetime (but didn't), who would you select?

If you were instantly able to play one musical instrument perfectly that you never have played before, what would it be?

If you were to be stranded forever on a tropical island with one platonic friend only, in whose company would you want to spend the rest of your days?

If you had to live the rest of your life in a place that you have never lived in before, where would you live?

If you could keep only one article of clothing you currently own and the rest were to be thrown out, what would you keep?

If you had to lose one of your five senses, which would you give up?

If you were to have one famous person alive or from history stranded with you on an island forevermore, who would you want it to be?

If you could kill the pet of anybody you know, whose pet would it be?

If you were to be recognized by posterity for one thing, what would you like to be known for?

If you could have said one sentence to Hitler while he was alive, what would you have said?

15

If you had to choose the color that describes you most accurately, which color would it be?

—·—  ≡✦≡  —·—

If you had to convert to a different religion, which would you choose?

—·—  ≡✦≡  —·—

If you were to drown in a liquid other than water, what would you want it to be?

—·—  ≡✦≡  —·—

If you could reverse one sports call in history, which one would it be?

If you had to name the most terrifying moment of your life so far, what would it be?

If you had to be homeless for one year, where would you want to be?

If you could have one street or square or park in any city or town renamed after you, which one would you select and exactly what would the name be?

If you could be guaranteed one thing in life besides money, what would you ask for?

**If** you could have one person alive today call you for advice, who would you want it to be?

---

**If** you could have any person from any time in history call you for advice, and they were to listen to what you told them, who would you want to hear from?

---

**If** you could easily visit one known planet, which one would you go to?

**If** you could have been the author of any single book already written, which book would you want to have penned?

If you could have any one specific power over other people, what would it be?

---

If you had to lose everyone you know in a tragic accident except one person, who would you choose to survive?

---

If you could have one meal from your past exactly as it was, which would you repeat?

---

If you could become famous for doing something that you don't currently do, what would it be?

If you could only keep one of your five senses, which would you save?

·—·  ≡✦≡  ·—·

If you could have lived during one period of time in past history, when and where would it be?

·—·  ≡✦≡  ·—·

If one by one, you had to place each of the people with you right now in another period of history that you think suits them best, when and where would you place them?

·—·  ≡✦≡  ·—·

If you had to describe the saddest thing that ever happened to you, what would you talk about?

20

If you had to spend one year alone in the wilderness, where would you go?

If you had to work in one type of factory for the remainder of your days but could choose which kind, what would you pick?

If you could possess one supernatural ability, what would it be?

If you had to paint your entire home, inside and out, a single color other than white, what color would you pick?

If you could have any single writer from history write your biography, who would it be?

❦

If you could have one current writer write your biography, who would you pick?

❦

If you could forever eliminate one specific type of prejudice from the earth, which would it be?

❦

If you could transport everyone you are with at this moment to another place, where would you all go?

22

If your home were to be totally destroyed by fire but you could save just one thing, what would it be?

---

If you were to have your friends, in private, attribute a single quality to you, what would you want it to be?

---

If you had to kill someone you know, who would it be, and how would you do it?

If a photograph of one part of your body were to be used in an advertisement, which part would you want to be used, and for what product or service?

If you could bring back any past leader of your country to run the country again, who would you want?

—— ≡◊≡ ——

If you could own any building in existence, which would you pick?

—— ≡◊≡ ——

If you could choose exactly what you will eat and drink for your last meal before death, what would the menu consist of?

If you could own any one existing sculpture from anywhere in the world, but not the right to ever sell it, which one would you want?

If you could make a gift of one thing to any single person alive today, who would it be, what would you give them, and how would you present it to them?

---

If you could have composed any single piece of music that already exists, which would you choose?

---

If you were invited to join one current musical group, which group would you want to be a member of, and what instrument would you play?

---

If you were to receive any existing public award, what award would you like to win?

If you could decide how to spend your last day alive, what would you do?

— ≡✦≡ —

If you could decide what will be written on your gravestone, what would you have inscribed?

— ≡✦≡ —

If you had to choose the single most valuable thing you ever learned, what would it be?

— ≡✦≡ —

If you were kidnapped and allowed to telephone one person for one minute only, who would you call?

26

**If** you could enact one law in your country that does not currently exist, what would it be?

***

**If** you could own only one thing for the rest of your life, what would you choose?

**If** you could be the current world champion in any one sport, which sport would it be?

***

**If** you could spend a weekend in any hotel in the world with all expenses paid, which hotel would you choose?

If you could cast an actor now alive to play you in a new film, what kind of film would it be and who would you choose?

If an actor no longer alive were to play you in a film, who would you cast in the role?

If you could have your portrait painted by any painter in history, to whom would you give the commission?

If you were given one hour to spend an unlimited amount of money in any store in the world, where would it be?

If you could say one sentence to the leader of the country you are presently in, what would you say?

---

If you had to choose the best advertising campaign ever created, which one would it be?

---

If you could have been any person from history, who would you want to have been?

---

If you could have a song written about you, what musician would you want to compose it, who would perform it, and what would it be called?

29

If you had to donate everything you own to a charity that you have never given to previously, which charity would you give to?

⊶ ⊷

If you could work for any person in the world, who would it be, and what job would you want?

⊶ ⊷

If you could discover one item that belonged to someone in history, whose would it be, and what would it be?

⊶ ⊷

If you could "uninvent" one thing in the world so that it would no longer exist, what would you choose?

30

If you were to be executed tomorrow but could decide the method, how would you prefer to go?

If you could play any position on your favorite sports team, what would it be?

If you could have a year any place in the world, all expenses paid, where would you go?

If you could see only one movie ever again, what film would you choose?

If you had to choose the title of your autobiography, what would it be?

If you could have only one piece of furniture in your house, what would you want it to be?

If you could have changed one thing about your first sexual experience, what would it be?

If you had to sleep with two famous people simultaneously, who would you choose?

If you could destroy a single tape or CD that your mate plays, what would it be?

⊹ ⚊⬦⚌ ⊹

If you could read the private diary of someone you know personally, whose diary would you read?

⊹ ⚊⬦⚌ ⊹

If you could read the diary of one person you don't know personally, whose would it be?

⊹ ⚊⬦⚌ ⊹

If you were on trial and someone you know (who is not a lawyer) had to act as your legal representative, who would you want to defend you?

If you could change one of your personality traits, what would it be?

— ≡✦≡ —

If you could adopt one personality trait from someone you know, what would you take, and from whom?

— ≡✦≡ —

If you could have a romance with any fictional character, who would it be?

— ≡✦≡ —

If you could have one person you know be your slave for one month, who would you choose?

34

If you could have avoided living one year from your past, which year would you like to have eliminated?

———— ❧ ————

If you could have the home phone number of anyone in the world, whose would it be, and what would you say to them?

If you could commit one crime without being caught, what crime would you commit?

———— ❧ ————

If you were kidnapped and could bring along only one personal possession, what would you take?

If you could be the parent of one famous person, who would you want it to be?

---

If you could ensure that your children never have one experience that you have had, what would it be?

---

If you could eat one food in any quantity for the rest of your life with no ill affects whatsoever, what food would you choose?

If you had to eliminate one season permanently (spring, summer, autumn, or winter), which one would go?

If you were going to initiate a new charity, what would be its mission and who would it benefit?

⊹ ⊱✦⊰ ⊹

If you could have been vice-president to any American president, which president would you choose?

⊹ ⊱✦⊰ ⊹

If you could "unknow" one thing you know, what would it be?

⊹ ⊱✦⊰ ⊹

If you could have one entire country "depopulated" as your private property, which country would you take as your own?

If you could have a secret camera in any one room in the world, what room would you put it in?

---

If you had to lose one of your limbs, which one would you sacrifice?

---

If you could only keep one of your limbs, which would you choose to keep?

---

If you were to have sex with two people simultaneously that you have known from your own past, who would you pick?

If you were to be the personal valet of any one man or woman from history, who would you want to work for?

If you could hire any architect alive or from history to design your dream house, who would you pick, and where would you build it?

If you could have invented anything from history, what would you pick?

If you could invent something that currently does not exist, what would it be?

If you could have been the first person to discover any part of the world, what place would you want to have found?

If you could have any music group alive today play at your birthday party, which group would you hire?

If you could have any music group that no longer exists play at your birthday party, who would you want?

If you could have a secret hideaway to escape to with a lover, where would it be?

If you were to cast the two romantic leads of a new film with any actors alive, who would you pick?

＋━ ≡◆≡ ━＋

If you could choose the way you will die, how would you want it to happen?

＋━ ≡◆≡ ━＋

If you could foresee a single day of your future in its entirety, what date would you select?

＋━ ≡◆≡ ━＋

If you had to have fought in any war in history, which would you have fought in?

If you could ask God any single question, what would it be?

---

If you could be one article of clothing, what would you be, and who would you want to belong to?

---

If you had to be someone's body part, what would you be, and on whose body?

---

If you were to be rescued from a desert island, by whom would you want to be rescued?

42

**If** you had to eat the same meal for the rest of your life, morning, noon, and night, without worrying about nutrition, what would you eat?

**If** you could live the life of any fictional character, which character would it be?

**If** you could have been any past president of the United States, who would you have been?

**If** you could have one person from history work for you as your personal assistant, who would it be?

If you could have the mind of someone you know but remain in your own body, whose brain would you take?

If you could have the mind of someone from history and remain in your own body, whose would you choose?

If you could coach any current sports team professionally, which would you choose?

If you had to name the single most regrettable thing about your country's history, what would it be?

If you could star in a love scene with any living actor, who would you want to act with, and where would you want it filmed?

⊱—⊰◆⊱—⊰

If you could have survived any historic disaster, which would you choose?

⊱—⊰◆⊱—⊰

If you could discover that something you thought was true was actually false, what would you wish it to be?

⊱—⊰◆⊱—⊰

If you could leave flowers on any one person's grave every week whether you knew them or not, who would it be?

45

If you could be invisible for one hour, where would you go and what would you do?

＊—＋ ≍✦≍ ＋—＊

If you could relive one romantic date from high school just as it was, which would it be?

＊—＋ ≍✦≍ ＋—＊

If you could relive one romantic date from high school as you would like it to have been, which would you choose?

＊—＋ ≍✦≍ ＋—＊

If you had to give up all sexual activity for one year, how much money would you demand (minimum) in return?

If you had to keep one part of your mate's body permanently in the freezer, what part would you save?

If you were the sole survivor of a plane crash with everyone present and had to choose someone to eat in order to survive, who would you select?

If you could eliminate one hereditary characteristic from your family, what would it be?

If you could be a student of any university in the world right now, where would you enroll?

If you could host a dinner party in any room in the world (without having to clean up), where would you want to have it?

⋯ ⋈⬧⋈ ⋯

If you could host a dinner party inviting any four people from history, who would you invite and where would the party take place?

⋯ ⋈⬧⋈ ⋯

If you were to be married to someone who is famous now, who would you pick to be your new spouse?

If you had to be married to someone famous from the past who is no longer alive, who would you like it to be?

If you had to have sex with someone that you know personally who is not of your sexually preferred gender, who would you select?

⋯⋯ ≍✦≍ ⋯⋯

If you could arrange a rock concert with any three musicians or groups to play on the same bill, who would you invite?

⋯⋯ ≍✦≍ ⋯⋯

If you could relive one single day from your past exactly as it was the first time, what day would you choose to experience all over again?

⋯⋯ ≍✦≍ ⋯⋯

If you could wake up tomorrow to learn that the major news-paper headlines were about you, what would you want them to say?

If you could eliminate one day from your past so that you had never had to live through it, which day would you erase?

—✦—

If you could go back in time, as yourself, to live for one year at any point in history, what year would you choose, and where would you go?

—✦—

If you could have had one composer from history write a symphony for you, who would it be?

—✦—

If you were to receive a letter today from anyone you have known during your lifetime, who would it be from and what would it say?

If you could have a telegram from one famous person now alive, who would it be from, and what would it say?

---

If you could have a telegram from one person from history, who would it be from and what would it say?

If one part of your body was to become a religious relic, which part would you like it to be?

---

If you were to be successful in another profession, what would you want to do?

If you could have been the architect of any one building in history, which building would you choose?

If you could have directed any film in history, what movie would it be?

If you had to spend all of your vacations for the rest of your life in the same place, where would you go?

If you were stranded on a desert island and could have with you only one object you currently own, what would you take?

52

If you won a lottery, what is the first thing you would do?

---

If you could have a secret listening device in any one room in the world, which room would you like it to be in?

---

If you had to inhabit the body of someone you know personally while keeping your own mind, whose body would you take?

---

If you could be a member of any club or association in the world, what would it be?

53

If you were given $5,000 to spend in one store in the world, where would you do your shopping?

If you could steal one thing in the world, other than money, without getting caught, what would you take?

If you could be the lover of any person alive other than your current lover, who would you pick?

If you could have been a lover of any person in history, who would you choose?

If you had to die in one of history's disasters, which one would you pick?

---

If you could take revenge on any person you have ever known, who would it be, why do they deserve it, and how would you do it?

---

If you were to perform in the circus, what would you do?

If you could master one type of cuisine, which one would you choose?

If you could be master chef in any restaurant in the world, where would you choose to cook?

If you could ensure that your child has one experience that you have had yourself, what would you want it to be?

If you could have a free telephone line to any one person in the world, who would it be?

If you could retract one lie you have told in your life, which would it be?

If you were stranded on a desert island and could have only one piece of music to listen to, what would it be?

If you were to die in a public place, exactly what spot would you choose?

If you were elected to be leader of a foreign country tomorrow, what country would you want it to be and what would be your first official act?

If you had to have one piece of music softly playing in your mind for the rest of your life, what would you want it to be?

57

If you had to have one family member (besides your spouse) witness your next sexual act, who would you pick?

---

If you could see anyone alive fully naked, who would you select?

---

If you could see one famous person from history fully naked, who would it be?

---

If you could be any sports figure now alive, who would you want to be?

If you were to give one person you know an award for something, who would it be, and for what?

If you had to choose someone with you right now to be president of the United States, who would you want it to be?

If you could become rich doing one thing that you currently don't do, what would you want it to be?

If you were to be a machine, what machine would you be?

If you could erase any one murder from history, which would it be?

If you had to change citizenship, which country would you want to become a citizen of?

If you could be married anywhere in the world, where would the wedding take place?

If you could be buried anywhere, where would it be?

If you could ensure one single personality trait in your children, what would you want it to be?

If you could run any single company, institution, or organization in the world, which would you choose?

If you had to select any single manmade object that best represents your personality, what would it be?

If you could gain total memory of one year of your life so far, which year would you pick?

61

If you could overthrow any government in the world, which one would you replace?

---

If you were to have a one-night stand with a current world leader, who would you choose?

---

If you were to bear the child of a famous person alive today, whose child would you like to have?

---

If you could have borne the child of a famous person no longer living, who would you choose?

62

If you could choose any historic figure to read your eulogy, who would you want to do it?

If you could call any person from history for advice tonight, who would you prefer to talk to?

If you could put anyone in prison, who would you lock up?

If you could undo one sexual encounter in your life so that it never happened, which one would it be?

If you could choose the music at your own funeral, what would it be, and who would play it?

⊷ ⊷ ≅✦≅ ⊶ ⊶

If you had to sleep with someone you despise in exchange for one thing, what is it that you would demand?

⊷ ⊷ ≅✦≅ ⊶ ⊶

If you had to spy on your own country for another country, which nation would you do it for?

If you had to name your single worst fear, what would it be?

**If** you had to describe the single worst thing a friend could do to you, what would it be?

**If** you were to invent an award to give to one commercial company, which one would you award, and for what?

**If** you could resolve any single dispute, anywhere in the world, what would you solve?

**If** you could be a contestant on any game show, which would you like to be on?

If you could read the mind of anyone you know, who would it be?

---

If you could read the mind of someone famous, who would it be?

---

If you could dance any one dance perfectly, which dance would you choose?

---

If you could be the editor of any single magazine, what publication would you pick?

If you were elected to be the leader of the United States tomorrow, what would be your first act?

If you could eliminate one thing you do each day in the bathroom so that you never had to do it again, what would it be?

If you had to have your mate get a part of their body pierced, exactly where would you want it to be?

If you could only hear one voice that you are familiar with for the rest of your life from the mouth of all people, whose would it be?

67

If you could serve in one capacity in the military (in which you haven't already served), what would you want to do?

—⟫✦⟪—

If you could eliminate forevermore one cause of death on earth, what would it be?

If you had to choose the best book in history, which book would get the prize?

—⟫✦⟪—

If you had to choose the worst book ever written, what would it be?

If you could use only one cosmetic item for the rest of your life, what would you choose?

---

If you could cure any disease, which would it be?

---

If you could be the owner of any current team in professional sports, which one would you want?

---

If you had to eliminate one odor from the earth, which one would you get rid of?

If you had to permanently give up your children to the care of someone you know, who would you wish it to be?

— ≡◆≡ —

If you had to give up your children to the care of someone famous, who would you pick?

— ≡◆≡ —

If you were to select a food that best describes your character, what food would it be?

— ≡◆≡ —

If you could arrange a jam session with any three musicians in history, who would you include?

70

**If** you could invent one new home appliance, what would it do?

**If** you were to be someone's personal computer, whose would you like to be?

**If** you were to be a news correspondent posted to any foreign country, where would you like to go?

**If** you had to choose a time in history when overall things were worse than any other single time, when would you say it was?

71

If you could take away the vocal chords of any person, who would it be?

≍

If you had to have one platonic friend witness your next sexual act, who would you ask?

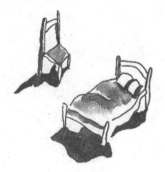

If you could be a guest on any television talk show, which would it be?

≍

If you were suddenly naked in front of everyone at work, what would you say to them?

If you could keep only one thing that is in your bathroom right now, as the only thing in there forever, what would you save?

⊶ ⚞⚟ ⊷

If you could have prevented one event in history, what event would you eliminate?

⊶ ⚞⚟ ⊷

If you had to rename your hometown, what would you call it?

⊶ ⚞⚟ ⊷

If you could teach your children only one lesson in life, what would it be?

73

If you had to be a member of another family you know, which family would you join?

***

If you had to cast living actors to play each of the people with you right now in a new film, who would you choose to play each person?

***

If you had to choose the worst work of art ever created, what would you choose?

***

If you had to choose the greatest work of art in history, what would you say is the best?

74

If you had the chance to make one purchase that you have passed up in your lifetime, what would it be?

If you had to describe your idea of the perfect mate, how would you do it?

If you could have been the producer of any single television show or series, which one would you pick?

If you could own any single newspaper in the world, which one would you pick?

If you could choose any six people to be the pallbearers at your funeral, who would you choose?

If you had to repeat your exact life over again exactly as it was, from any age, what age would you go back to?

If you could find one thing, besides money, in your family attic, what would you want to discover?

If you could go back to any age and start a different life, what age would that be?

If you had to eliminate a single art form from the earth henceforth and forevermore, which one would you get rid of?

If you had to name the single most important quality of a good mate, what would it be?

If the world could henceforth have only one single art form, what do you think it should be?

If you had been the original designer of one existing corporate logo, which one would you select?

77

If you could wear only one color, besides white or black, for the rest of your life, what would you wear?

If you had to eat in only one restaurant for the rest of your life, which one would you choose?

If you had to be represented by an object in your home, what would you choose?

If you could have changed any one thing about the death of one of your relatives, what would you alter?

78

If you had been the reporter to have broken one news event during your lifetime, what would you like it to have been?

If you could have any type of fresh cut flowers delivered to your home every week, what one type would you pick?

If you had to be the underwear of someone famous, who would you choose to wear you?

If you could have refereed one sports match in history, which one would you pick?

If you could put a new tattoo on someone you know, who would you pick, what would it be, and where would you put it?

⊷ ☰✦☰ ⊶

If you could make someone else live one moment from your own life, who would you select, and what moment?

⊷ ☰✦☰ ⊶

If you could keep only one home appliance, which would you keep?

If you were to be reincarnated as an animal, what kind would you want to be?

If you could ask a single question of a dead relative, what would it be and of whom would you ask it?

---

If you could have changed one thing about your parents while you were a child, what would it have been?

---

If you had to have a personal friend redecorate your house, who would you pick to do it?

---

If you could give a single piece of advice to the film industry in Hollywood, what would you say?

If you had to rename each of the people you are with right now, what would you call each of them?

If you had to marry someone that you presently know un-romantically, and spend the rest of your life as their spouse, who would you choose?

If you had to choose one country in the world other than the United States to become the only superpower of the twenty-first century, which country would you pick?

If you had to choose one person currently in the U.S. government to control the nuclear forces instead of the president, who would it be?

If you could choose both major candidates for the next United States presidential race, what two people would you pick?

＊＊＊＊＊

If you could have worked for anyone in history, in your own field, who would you choose?

＊＊＊＊＊

If you could have been the person who discovered any country in history, which country would you like to have been the first to find?

If you had to cancel one hour of the day, every day, which hour would you eliminate?

If you could go back in time, as yourself, to observe any single event from history, what would you want to witness?

***

If you were to choose a musical instrument that best describes your character, what would it be?

If you had to exchange one physical attribute with someone in the room, who would you pick, and what would you exchange with them?

***

If you had to cancel one month of the year forevermore, so that period of time no longer existed, which month would go?

If you could choose one new symbol for your family crest, what would it be?

---

If you could do any job in the world for one day, what would it be?

---

If you could be anywhere in history for one day, as someone famous from that time, where would you like to be, when, and as who?

---

If you had to choose the best television show ever made, which one would you pick?

85

If you could have been any sports figure from history, who would you want to have been?

---

If you could change one thing about your life, what would it be?

---

If you had to choose the prize for the best movie in history, what film would win?

---

If you had to pick the worst movie in history, which one would get the dubious honor?

If you could practice only one of the principle vices henceforth, which one would you stick with?

---

If you could have discovered one medical cure in history, which one would you choose?

If you could have sued any one person in your life, who would it be, and for what?

---

If you could have been a jury member in any court case in history, which trial would you choose?

If you had to murder someone, how would you do it?

If you had to commit suicide by jumping from a tall height, where would you do it?

If you could choose the very last thing you will see before death, what would it be?

If you had to trade houses with someone you know, who would it be?

If you had to have been any dictator or tyrant in history, which one would you choose to have been?

---

If you could add one sentence to the U.S. Constitution, what would it say?

---

If you could bomb one building in the world without hurting any people, which would you blow up?

---

If you could be the author of any one quotation from history, what words would you like to have uttered?

89

If you had to confess to one crime you have already committed, what would you confess to?

⊶ ≡✦≣ ⊷

If you could choose, from what you own right now, what clothes to be buried in when you die, what would you wear?

⊶ ≡✦≣ ⊷

If you had to describe the worst job interview in your life, what job would it have been for?

⊶ ≡✦≣ ⊷

If you could have hit any homerun in baseball history, which one would you choose?

**If** you were to be any famous person's personal masseuse, whose would you like to be?

---

**If** you could give anonymous advice to any one person about their appearance, who would it be, and what would you say?

---

**If** you could be on the cover of any magazine next month, which magazine would you want it to be, and what would the caption say?

**If** you had to pick the worst meal you've ever eaten, what would it be?

If everything in the world had to have the same odor, what scent would you want it to be?

---

If you could give your parents one gift, what would you give them?

If you were to receive one honorary degree in your lifetime, which university would you prefer, and for what accomplishment?

---

If you could have given one speech in history, which one would you pick?

If you could have been on the United States Supreme Court for any single case in its history, which would you select?

---

If you could physically strike one person from your past (that you didn't), who would you hit, and where?

---

If you could change one election result from the past so that the loser had won, which one would it be?

---

If you had to die from something other than old age, how would you prefer to go?

If you had to name the worst job in the world, what would it be?

——— ✠ ———

If you could own the entire wardrobe of any one television character, from the show they're on, whose clothes would you want?

——— ✠ ———

If you could cancel one vacation you have taken, lose all memory of it, and get your money back, what vacation would you choose?

——— ✠ ———

If you had to choose the worst work experience you've ever had, what would you pick?

If you could cancel forever a single thing you have to do every day other than your job, what would it be?

If you had to go tonight to be tattooed, where on your body would you have it done and what image would you select?

If you could realize a dream that you have had while asleep, what dream would you pick?

If you could choose only one color and image for your country's new flag, what would it look like?

If you had to identify the worst hotel room you have ever stayed in, where was it?

⊶ ⧓ ⊷

If you had to name the most important invention in history, what would win?

If you had to describe the best kiss you've ever had, how would you describe it?

⊶ ⧓ ⊷

If your house were to be haunted by the ghost of one person from history, who would you wish it to be?

If you had to choose the best song ever composed, which one would it be?

If you had to choose the worst song ever composed, which one would you pick?

If you had to change your race, what would you want to be?

If you had to select the most beautiful face in history, whose face would you pick?

97

If you had to pick the worst sexual experience of your life, what would it be?

If you could solve one unsolved crime, which one would you solve?

If you were to be renamed after someone from history, whose name would you want?

If you could accomplish only one thing in the rest of your life, what would it be?

If you could have the sex life of any person from history, but remain yourself, who would you choose?

If you could have anyone's eyes in the world, whose eyes would you want?

If you could completely eliminate one of your pet peeves, what would you get rid of?

If you could win any competition in the world, what would it be for?

**If** you had to choose the worst telephone call you've ever had, what call was it?

**If** you had to choose the best telephone call you've ever had, which was it?

—— ⋈ ——

**If** you could have the hair of someone you know, whose would you take?

—— ⋈ ——

**If** you had to serve a life sentence in jail for one crime, what crime would you commit?

If you just learned that you had exactly one year to live, what would you do with your remaining time?

---

If you were to have only one of the prime virtues, which one would you want to possess?

---

If you could break one current world sports record, which one would it be?

---

If you had to recall the worst date you've ever been on, which one was it?

If you were to permanently give up sex for one thing other than money, what would you do it for?

———— ⬦ ————

If you could tell your boss one thing with complete impunity, what would you say?

———— ⬦ ————

If you could have prevented one natural disaster that actually happened, what would it be?

———— ⬦ ————

If you could hold one position in current government, what would you want to do?

102

If your plane was about to crash and you had time to write one quick note, to whom would you write, and what would you say?

If you were to adopt an orphan from another country, which country would the child come from?

If you were to pick a moment in history when, all things considered, the world was better off, which would it be?

If you could change one thing to make life easier for your own gender, what would you change?

If you were allowed to eat only one vegetable for the rest of your life, which one would it be?

If you could change the ending of any book ever written, which one would you pick and how would you change it?

If you had to spend one weekend alone in a single store but could remove nothing, which store would you pick?

If you could referee or judge one sport as a permanent job, which would you choose?

If you could give a single piece of advice to the automobile industry, what would you tell them?

If you had to choose someone to sleep with your mate, who would you pick?

If you had to sacrifice your own life for one thing, what would it be?

If you had to repeat one alcohol or drug experience you've had, which one would you relive?

105

If you could see through the clothes of any one person at all times, who would it be?

—————— ✠ ——————

If you could call any living person to ask for advice tonight, who would you call?

—————— ✠ ——————

If you could recover one thing you've lost in your lifetime, what would you wish to find?

—————— ✠ ——————

If you could memorize one book from history in its entirety, which book would you want it to be?

106

If you could make a sequel to any movie you have ever seen, which one would it be?

If you were given a yacht today, what would you name it?

If you were given a racehorse, what would you name it?

If you had to name the best purchase you've ever made, which one would you choose?

If you could spend one year looking for one thing in the world, what would you search for?

---

If you had written one song from this century yourself, which would you like to have written?

---

If you could have been told one thing that you weren't told when you were a teenager, what would you like to have heard?

If you were sentenced to spend the rest of your life in a prison cell with one person you know, who would you take?

108

If you could pick one famous person to be your neighbor, who would you have next door to you?

⋯ ≓✦≓ ⋯

If you could live on any one street in the world, which address would you choose?

⋯ ≓✦≓ ⋯

If you could sing any one song beautifully and perfectly, which one would you pick?

⋯ ≓✦≓ ⋯

If you were going to turn to crime to support yourself from now on, what kind of criminal would you become?

If you could occupy the world described in a novel, which would you choose?

If you could change one thing about your home, what would you make different?

If you could make one fairytale or fable come true with yourself in it, which would you pick?

If you could teach a person any single thing, who and what would you choose?

If you had to cancel one day of the week forever, which day would go?

If you could break one world's record for anything other than sports, what would it be?

If you had to choose the worst home you've ever lived in, which one was it?

If you could be the only one to hear the confession of one criminal from history, who would it be?

If you had to choose the most important single event of this century, what would win the honor?

---

If you could leave a time capsule the size of a microwave oven to be found centuries from now, what would you put inside it?

If you were asked what to put in a new breakfast cereal box as a gimmick, what would you pick?

---

If you had to secretly dispose of a dead body, how would you do it?

If you could be forgiven for one thing in your life, what would you choose?

If you had to predict the most important development of the twenty-first century, what do you think it will be?

If you could only have sex once more in your life, when would you do it, with whom, and where?

If you could romantically kiss someone that you never have, who would you want it to be?

If you could keep your mate but have the rest of the world populated by only one gender, which would it be?

If you could have a voodoo doll that functioned for one person you know, who would that person be, and what would you use it for?

If you could change one thing about your city or town or neighborhood, what would you alter?

If you could firebomb any store or business, which would you do it to?

114

If you had to pick the most important quality for a leader of your country, what would it be?

If you could change the ending to one movie you have seen, which one would it be, and how would you reshoot it?

If you could reverse the effects of any one environmental problem that we are currently faced with, what problem would you choose to mend?

If you could, in retrospect, have purchased a large quantity of stock the day it was first issued, which one would it have been?

If you had to choose the single biggest mistake you have made in life so far, what would it be?

━━ ≖✦≖ ━━

If you could throw a party in any existing interior space in the world, where would you have it?

━━ ≖✦≖ ━━

If you could arrange for any two singers to record a duet together, which two would you pick, and what song would you have them sing?

If you had to describe your worst medical experience, what would it be?

If you could give anonymous advice to one set of parents you know about how they are raising their kids, who would it be and what would you tell them?

---

If you could go back in time just long enough to tell the founding fathers of America one thing, what would you tell or warn them of?

---

If you could eliminate one habit your mate has, what would you have them stop doing?

---

If you had to spend one weekend alone in a single public building or institution, which building would you choose?

If you could have one current politician removed from office, who would you get rid of?

— ✠ —

If you had to name one thing that your mate could do to assure that you would leave them forever, what would it be?

— ✠ —

If you could eliminate one habit you have, what would you stop doing?

— ✠ —

If you just learned that you were to die in exactly one hour, what would you do?

118

If you had to drop a nuclear bomb on one country, where would you drop it?

⋅⋅→⋅ ▆◆▆ ⋅←⋅⋅

If you could have witnessed any biblical event, what would you want to have seen?

⋅⋅→⋅ ▆◆▆ ⋅←⋅⋅

If you could work for any corporation for which you don't currently work, which would you choose?

⋅⋅→⋅ ▆◆▆ ⋅←⋅⋅

If your own ashes were to be kept in an urn, after you die, where would you want the urn kept?

If you could plan the perfect evening out, what would it involve?

---

If you could program the perfect evening of television shows, which ones would you select, and in what order?

---

If you had to kill one person you work with, who would you off?

If you had to name the dumbest purchase you've ever made, which would it be?

If you could receive all the products from a single company for free (but could not resell them), which company would you choose?

⋯ ≡✦≡ ⋯

If you had to name the one thing that makes you angriest about a relative, what would it be?

⋯ ≡✦≡ ⋯

If you were to become the sex slave of one person from history, who would you want it to be?

⋯ ≡✦≡ ⋯

If you had to describe the perfect body, what would you say about it?

121

If you could have the autograph of one person from history, who would it be?

If you could have any view from your home, what would it be of?

If you could have asked Richard Nixon one thing, what would you have asked?

If you could have the world's largest collection of one thing, what would it be?

122

If you could have been the hero from any war, which war would it be, and for what heroic deed?

If you were to inhabit the world of any video or computer game, which one would you select?

If you could leave only one existing book for the world to have five hundred years from now (other than this one), which book would you leave?

If you just learned that tomorrow morning you were to be permanently exiled from your country and could take just three things with you, what would they be?

If you could teach your pet to do one thing, what would it be?

⟶ ⋝◆⋜ ⟵

If you could teach your mate to do one thing, what would it be?

If you could write letters to only one person for the rest of your life, who would receive them?

⟶ ⋝◆⋜ ⟵

If you were to be reincarnated as someone you know, who would it be?

124

If you were to be given an acting role in a current TV show, who would you want to play?

If you could arrange for one thing to befall your boss, what would you have happen?

If you could start a new rock band, what would you name it?

If you could have a servant come to your house every day for one hour, what would you have them do?

125

If you were to have your portrait painted, what would you choose as the setting?

＊ ＊ ＊

If you could choose the very last thing you would see before you die, what would it be?

＊ ＊ ＊

If you were to be cremated, where would you want your ashes scattered?

＊ ＊ ＊

If you had to choose your best sexual experience, what would it be?

126

If you could, it retrospect, thank one teacher you had in school for what they taught you, who would it be, and what would you thank them for?

If you had to pick the worst television series ever made, what would win?

＋・ ━◆━ ・＋

If you could reverse the ongoing extinction of any animal now endangered, which animal would you choose to save?

＋・ ━◆━ ・＋

If you could make a film from any book never produced as a film, what book would you pick?

If you could change one thing to make life easier for your children, what would you do?

---

If you had to sell your soul for one thing, what would it be?

---

If you could achieve absolute success in only one area of your life, what would you want it to be?

---

If you could determine the careers of your children, what would you have them do, assuming they would be successful at it?

128

If you could visit only one more place in the world that you have never been, where would you go for this final voyage?

If you could have anyone locked in a room so that you could torment them for a day, who would you choose, and how would you torment them?

If you had to pick the most difficult question you could be asked, what would it be?

If you could have the answer to any question, what would you ask?

## About the Authors

Evelyn McFarlane was born in Brooklyn and grew up in San Diego. She received her degree in architecture from Cornell University in 1985, and has lived and worked in Boston, New York, and Syracuse. She is currently living and working in Florence, Italy, teaching design for Syracuse University. She has an architectural practice with her partner, Adam Drisin. When she is not working, she spends her time traveling in Italy, painting, and renovating a small house in a medieval hill town in Umbria. This is her first book.

James Saywell was born in 1959 in Toronto, Canada. He lived in Hong Kong and China as a child. His travels through Asia at a young age instilled in him a passion for architecture, which he eventually studied in Toronto and Princeton. He lived and worked in the United States for eight years until moving to Florence, Italy, in 1993 to teach architecture. He divides his time between designing furniture for his company, Stillworks Inc., architecture, teaching, and learning to paint. He lives in a farmhouse in Tuscany. This is his first book.